Recognizing
THE GIFTS
IN THE WOUND
(The Lessons of Being Human)

BRIAN ROSCOE

Recognizing THE GIFTS IN THE WOUND

"It takes courage to love, but pain through love is the purifying fire which those who love generously know. We all know people who are so much afraid of pain that they shut themselves up like clams in a shell and, giving out nothing, receive nothing and therefore shrink until life is a mere living death."
-Eleanor Roosevelt

There are moments in this life when we get to a place where we can see very clearly that this world, and our experience in it, is created to assist our journey, not limit it. Virtually everything that happens can be used and seen as a mechanism for growth. And behind the phrase, "You just can't mind that sometimes life hurts," we come to the understanding that our physical, emotional and spiritual pain, in its base nature, will always bring a quality of unexpected growth in our journey. We endure it, we embrace our opportunity, acknowledging but not being owned by the pain, and we learn from it.

Allowing our pain to simply be what it is, and not minding the human experience of it, not remolding it into chronic suffering, we can always find a way to grow through it. We get to that place within ourselves that we understand that, yes, indeed, there is discomfort, there are wounds in this life, and when we find that understanding, we open ourselves up, crack the doors of our heart, and we find gifts, often gold we never expected behind all that irritation, all that pain, all that anguish. And it's here that we're privileged to touch the infinite qualities of wisdom hiding behind that wound that we thought would only leave an ugly scar in our soul. In truth, it helped uncover our soul, open our heart and remember our truth… gold.

Recognizing THE GIFTS IN THE WOUND

> Be the *gift* you were made
> to be anywhere you find
> yourself, and don't ever let
> the world convince you that
> your *Truth* does not exist
> wherever you are.

Allow yourself to be formed through the inevitable difficulties, the rifts, knots, and flaws that exist in this life. See them like we see flaws in a beautiful piece of wood. It's the knots that make that wood interesting, the twisting of the grain that draws us in to look closer, and all its imperfections are far more beautiful once a finish is applied. I think the same is true for us. We just need to be finished off properly, healed in our hearts. It allows our grain to glow. And yeah, we can always use a dusting, or occasionally another coat of varnish, but that's just the nature of being dynamic and human. That's the nature of life.

All experience is simply meant to be a reminder of who we can be, and we can always choose to be the best of that. Because, really, we're allowing ourselves to be reminded of what and who we already are, and the experience of life, good or bad, pleasant or difficult, only touches on and draws that out of us. Often, experiences are our wake up call, and there's not a moment on this earth that's not designed with the potential to bring us closer to ourselves. It's up to us to find and lean into that *potential*.

Recognizing THE GIFTS IN THE WOUND

To find courage is to explore the opportunity to be that which we learned to believe we could not be. Claiming our courage requires us to explore living and expanding beyond our fear despite ourselves, and to move towards the life we know we're meant for—the life we want to create.

Over time, as we open our hearts up to truth at any cost, we begin to realize that what we've been looking at as our wounds are not, but are the stories we've made up about what we believe our wounds to be.

We'll always miss the gift in the wound when we stubbornly insist on looking at it through an old dirty lens. Like an old movie camera, we need to change our focus, find a lens more suited to our spirit.

The wound you think you're looking at is never the actual truth of the wound. You're looking at the reflection of your wound, often a distortion. You're stuck in a story that you've made up in your mind in order to egotistically negotiate your pain, the one you've become obsessed with that you think is the problem, but is not. Rather, open yourself up to its deeper meaning, its message and healing, in whatever form that takes. The truth of the wound does

Recognizing THE GIFTS IN THE WOUND

not come easily to us. It's not meant to. It requires work, the cultivation of fresh thought through you, and the purity of love in order for a true healing to occur. And the bottom line is always if you're still feeling the same pain and suffering, you haven't approached it with the spirit of who you're meant to be.

Keep in mind, our wounds are not only from this life, but brought forward from the wounds of our parents and from their parents. We're here to heal that, and to heal the future perception of wounds experienced by our children and theirs.

> *"When we argue for our limitations,*
> *we get to keep them."*
> *-Evelyn Waugh*

ROSCOE

When we refuse to change the things that have stagnated generations of our families, to look within ourselves for the secrets that can change the world, we fail those we love, including ourselves.

Recognizing THE GIFTS IN THE WOUND

When you find yourself stuck in difficult circumstances, sometimes it helps to give yourself a little space from them, to step back and observe them rather than immediately reacting into them. Spend time identifying all the feelings, the fear, the personalization, the hurt and tender injury of the situation. Acknowledge it just enough to be present in its discomfort, but without becoming that discomfort. Question the truth of your feelings and observe yourself in the process.

Stepping aside from the mind's tendency to have to figure-it-out-now helps you open up to a clearer thinking and allows you to avoid the wallowing-in-your-anxiety experience. It allows you to seek out what might be behind the struggle, to look for understanding rather than living in the anguish of it.

ROSCOE

You may not have created
the world, but you are
co-creator of your *world*.

So where do you want to
go with that one, tiger?!

Recognizing THE GIFTS IN THE WOUND

Struggle always leads me into questioning my values and opening myself to a recalibration of my belief systems. I like that. I don't care for the struggle part, but I do like the transformation that inevitably unfolds. Sometimes I just have to smile at it, acknowledge what it is, and remember they're all just thoughts, and, like all thoughts, they hold the potential to point you toward universal truths when given a chance. And they'll continuously present themselves until we're ready to really hear them and see our life in new ways.

There's a power in questioning your life. It's through the struggle of determining which belief systems hold value and truth, and which require our disposal, that we find the wisdom and the freedom to be ourselves.

There will always be times in our lives that feel hard and difficult to endure. Sometimes I simply have to step back and center on

the phrase: "This is simply life unfolding as *[whatever the feelings or experience is]*."

For example: Right now, this is life unfolding as… a loss of someone I love, or a feeling of heartbreak, or financial stress, or kids driving me crazy… The list really is endless. But it frees me up a little, takes the anxious charge of the situation down a bit, allowing me to continue on the journey that my heart asks of me—the journey of opening to my world and everything it offers without getting trapped in it. It helps me embrace my experience of being fully human.

So your *"unfolding statement"* could look something like:

"This is simply life unfolding as me feeling *a particular emotion* about *a particular problem,*" or, "This is simply life unfolding as a *human situation.*"

Examples:

- "This is life unfolding around what it is to find a scratch on my car."
- Or, "This is life unfolding as watching the birds outside."
- Or, "This is life unfolding as a horrible divorce."
- Or, "This is life unfolding as driving in snow, flying on a plane, being on a cruise."
- Or, "This is life unfolding as finding joy in being a parent, spouse, friend."
- Or, "This is life unfolding as what it is to be employed or have a business."

We can use it anywhere, we can use it to *appreciate the moment* or to help quiet it. The point is to get yourself out of the overwhelm of an experience and into observing life from a place where you can be more present to what's happening, see the *beauty and complexity of the miracle*, view your life experience and everything that unfolds in a healthier, more rational, and hopefully more enjoyable way.

Recognizing THE GIFTS IN THE WOUND

"If you're really listening, if you are awake to the poignant beauty of the world, your heart breaks regularly. In fact, your heart is made to break; its purpose is to burst open again and again so that it can hold evermore (life's enormous) wonders."
-*Andrew Harvey*

When it comes to life, conflict, difficulty, joy, happiness, irritation… anything human, you never walk away empty. There's always a gift. When you choose to open that gift, explore what it is for you, your part in it is up to you. It may take moments, it may be decades before you even know its purpose or that it even exists, but it's always there waiting for your work, your understanding. The gifts that come through being alive and human are forever present to us. Stay open.

Scared to see or express our vulnerability, we become a prisoner of our programmed beliefs about the very thing we fear: our vulnerability. We live never questioning how we got there, avoiding answers that feel threatening to us. There's an irony in the fact that we're here to see and know ourselves, to find our strength and understand love, that's our journey. And we stay on this path to ourselves despite the fact that we know this life is fraught with fear and feelings of vulnerability. Tenacious, the human spirit is a tenacious one.

> **A man who's scared to see or express his own *vulnerability* is a prisoner of society and his own evolution, or perhaps lack of *evolution*.**

Everything feels worse when perceived through fear.

QUESTIONS AND RUMINATIONS FOR THE JOURNEY

We have a choice: to perceive our lives through a lens of fear, or to see life in a bigger way, through a lens centered through the heart, one that's expansive rather than contracting, opening us up to the world and not suffocating our souls.

Explore this for yourself. What's your best lens to see your experience through? What's your brightest way to see your world, what quality of thought creates the greatest clarity when it comes to living your truth? Have you figured out how to open up to your world so you

Recognizing THE GIFTS IN THE WOUND

can live your love? Have you experienced the essential nature of *you* through your heart?

We know which lenses don't work—the lens of anxiety, self-doubt, and worry. They only influence and strengthen our lenses of fear. Our objective is to move toward peace, to move towards the lenses of love, non-judgment, kindness, and gratitude. These are far more appropriate for our true goal. And our work is to fit ourselves with these lenses of awareness and vision. To figure out what quality of consciousness and thought best serves our heart, and, from there, how can we best love ourselves and one another.

GOING OFF-ROAD WITH SELF-DESTRUCTIVE THINKING

"Happiness is an attitude. We either make ourselves miserable or happy and strong. The amount of work is the same."
-Francesca Reigler

When I feel the urge to participate in a fear-based thought and/or actions of any kind, I pretty much know I'm stuck inside my head, I know that I'm believing in habits of the mind that inevitably lead me into something disappointing or at the very least distracting from living my life. I know it's a stuckness

Recognizing THE GIFTS IN THE WOUND

because it stands to reason that the quality of my thinking dictates my actions, so it goes without saying that if I'm participating in actions that are off center, then, prior to that, my thinking was off center, and when I realize that, I have power. Granted, realizing all this and taking the appropriate detour before driving off the cliff would have proven more fruitful, but next time!

Next time, I'll nip it!

Note to self: When my actions or thoughts leave me feeling outside myself, not peaceful, not grounded, I know I need to step away and re-boot myself back toward balance. Taking these steps toward peace helps me nurture my truth and not waste my time here, wallowing in the dark habits of the mind.

"We need to remember that circumstances don't make a person, they reveal a person."
-Emma Jameson

Our hearts are made to be broken, and it's in our healing process that we remember who we are; it's here that we earn our ability to walk forward with truth, heart first, confidently, to walk knowing that we are both vulnerable and strong, and that beginning again is part of our strength. It's a strength that doesn't overwhelm. It simply means we have remembered and we've fought for our ability to love, to understand, and to hold ourselves and one another without compromising that love when difficult and fearful thoughts present.

JOURNEY PROMPT

What thoughts most pull you from your love? What pulls you toward it? Which do you prefer?

Recognizing THE GIFTS IN THE WOUND

"Your work is to discover your world, and then, with all your heart, give yourself to it."
-The Buddha

Simply being on this human journey automatically sets us up for amazing potential for growth we could've never designed by ourselves. We're constantly pointed back toward ourselves until lessons are learned and self-love is rekindled. Made vulnerable to this world, we endure the anguish, the pain, and the suffering of the journey, and it brings with it an entire system of self-analysis, evaluation, resolution and, on a good day, wisdom.

So, honor your torment! Because it's through our torment, pain, suffering, laying in our burnt-out, crust-laden life experience that we become inspired to move forward. This is where we're challenged by the, *"There's got to be more than this to life!"* or, *"Nope, not doing that!"* internal exchange within our lives. It's through our bewilderment and confusion with life's path that we're pushed to seek a deeper understanding behind the pain; here, we look for the identity of our human expression, and finally seek out the tree of life, where our original seed sprang. So, hold your struggles lovingly. They can help guide your way home.

JOURNEY PROMPT

Every challenge or difficult time that you've successfully navigated through helps define who you are, has pushed you into becoming your better you, or helped you touch a place of wisdom within. That's just how the warrior's journey works. You may never care for the struggle of life, but would you really want to give back its gifts?

"With everything that has happened to you, you can either feel sorry for yourself or treat what has happened as a gift. Everything is either an opportunity to grow or an obstacle to keep you from growing. You get to choose."
-Wayne W. Dyer

Even now, as you hold your breath, angry, frustrated, sad, and ready to explode... *Welcome* to your journey!

We all have our moments when we're questioning the journey, times when we feel like we just want our life back, but it is all part of our journey. All of our experiences are expressions of our life. Whether you're experiencing tragedy or joy, resentment or appreciation, it all sets you up to step forward, to be present and participate in your journey. The journey is always there, but the quality of your participation is up to you.

Recognizing THE GIFTS IN THE WOUND

Our higher self is not as concerned with our pain as it is with our *growth*.

Loss is never easy, but we're always offered a growth and a freedom through our loss and difficulty that we would not and could not have chosen on our own.

On a higher level, a level more of the spirit than of the mind, there's help directing us into our journey. Choices get made at higher levels that impact our human lives, life gets directed and unfolds perfectly for us to complete our journey in the most productive way. The pain is of little concern. The outcome, the finished (but not completely finished) product is what's important.

So, perhaps, some of the difficult things in life come to us with a hidden but higher intention from spirit, and there are reasons for everything besides simply causing us disruption; that through an agreement made from our higher and more spirited connection, a connection we've all been created with, and one that our minds are incapable of ever completely understanding, we are presented with exactly what we need at the appropriate time by a teacher who is not concerned with our pain, only the perfect lessons for our growth. This teacher knows pain is temporary and fleeting, but that our growth is forever. So many of our greatest lessons are ones we could not have organized on our own—issues and struggles we could not have known the consequences and value of and, in our human way, we could not and would not steer ourselves into. So, we're given a sort of cohort for the journey to make sure we're not wasting our time here!

Recognizing THE GIFTS IN THE WOUND

Regardless of the origin of our pain,
we need to ask ourselves:
how can I best embrace this challenge to change?

JOURNEY PROMPT

Remember: Life doesn't so much care about your pain. Life cares about your growth. Things don't come to you over and over and over again so that you can put them in a drawer. They come to you because they want to be healed.

We just need to step up and say, "Okay, I'm ready. What do I need to do in order to bring healing and love to this situation?"

That opens up a whole new can of worms! But that's what we are—we're all a bunch of worm-can openers! We just need to pick a good can!

When we're embroiled in difficulties and drama with one another, it's pretty hard to see a bigger picture in that moment. It might not seem like it in the moment, but we're all actually working towards a bigger goal together, because behind all the turmoil exists solutions, and the deeper truth is found through reclaiming our peace. This is a choice. We have to choose to look for peace, and when we do, its gifts are abundant.

Through our mistakes and turmoil, we're subconsciously offering each other opportunities to recognize what we don't want our life to be and, in that, we give ourselves and one another a chance to imagine something different and the ability to claim personal freedom. It's in these difficulties, in the pain we inflict on ourselves and one another, that, unbeknownst to us, we co-create the circumstances that inspire us to look for and find a better way. We're offering one another peace, even if we end up fighting to find it. We very well may habitually follow this pattern until we realize that we can do it without the drama and trauma part. We can reclaim our heart, and find fresh thought, a new way to be, through a centered breath and a well-placed intention.

> *"Everything can be taken from a man but one thing: the last of the human freedoms— to choose one's attitude in any given set of circumstances, to choose one's own way."*
> *-Viktor E. Frankl*

JOURNEY PROMPT

Ever get so caught up in the drama of a problem that you couldn't even begin to see a solution? It's almost a redundant question, because we all do it. So, when you do that, when you're stuck in a problem, unable to think about anything else, how does that feel? What does it look like when you're doing that? What do you think of yourself? Who do you become? Can you see how your thinking and behavior aligns with being stuck in your problems? Try to step back from everything and view it from a renewed point of view or attitude.

Recognizing THE GIFTS IN THE WOUND

Being stuck can feel pretty horrible, and it gets really old after a while. Give yourself permission to start over, to find a way that allows you to experience the wonderful things about yourself, not to mention the ability to find beautiful, healthy solutions to whatever is happening around you. This can be a much more productive way to live. Remember that, at any point in time, we could just be stuck in an anxious thought, and change is always only one thought away.

> **Don't allow fear to dictate the quality of your *presence* and *participation* in this world.**

Understand that no matter what you need to endure in this life, you are strong and were made to heal. No matter what struggles emerge that make you feel separate and alone, you're made to be here, made to be in a great embrace with life. Your presence in this world is a gift, and your destiny is love. It's the way you approach what comes to and through you that will define the quality of your experience and your influence on the experience of others.

Recognizing THE GIFTS IN THE WOUND

JOURNEY PROMPT

Consider two things you can do this week, things that are natural to you, a real part of your true nature, that both enhance your experience and positively influence the experience of others. (It's okay to surprise people with your choices. Those choices may be a part of you they don't know, but should.)

1)

2)

In approaching our vulnerability, we open to our humanness, and in that place, where we can admit our struggles, we find a strength within us that only appears by embracing the deeper truth of who we are. We are all vulnerable.

When we're scared to look at and interact with our vulnerability, we become a prisoner of our fear, a prisoner of the world's brainwashing and, more importantly, we end up a prisoner of our own faulty beliefs. refusing to be who we are.

We think that feeling vulnerable is weak or to be avoided and has no value, but nothing could be further from the truth. We need our vulnerability to truly know love, and, through that, we automatically know ourselves.

This is an unsure human moment, and I will *grow* from it.

"Vulnerability is uncertainty, risk, and emotional exposure. Though scary, it's also a powerful and authentic way to live. Vulnerability is the core, the heart, the center, of meaningful human experiences."
-Brené Brown

Recognizing THE GIFTS IN THE WOUND

Understanding life, in its many shades of emotion, can be all this and more: painful, insecure, heartbreaking, shameful, unstable, as well as loving, joyful, creative, successful, empathetic, and kind. Life allows us to experience what it is to be vulnerable and come out stronger and wiser from it. When you're no longer controlled by your fear of the pain and uncertain struggle in life, when you accept what life is, knowing that your vulnerability in the world is a very real part of your truth, it no longer has control over you because you no longer see yourself as broken. In this, we find a quality of strength and life that helps maintain a certain quality of peace in all our unsure moments.

SEE THE LESSON.
LOVE THE FEAR.

*Nothing ever goes away until it
teaches us what we need to know."
-Pema Chodron*

This is a big one! How do we love our pain, especially the emotional stuff? How do you love something that seems like all it wants to do is drain you? The same is true for fear. How do you love the fear that is so dedicated to keeping you away from your true nature? And why would you want to put all that effort into loving either of these trouble makers?

Recognizing THE GIFTS IN THE WOUND

Answer? Because resisting them doesn't work. Our resistance gets us nowhere. We need to lean into and even have gratitude for our struggles and all the lessons held in them. Because when you love something, you release it, and, in that, you refuse its power over you while, at the same time, you can open up to its gifts. What you resist feeds on that resistance. It sucks more life from you than you're willing to admit as you're fighting for your stance, your idea, or belief. In approaching our struggles with love, we release ourselves from the influence of resisting and simply open to the lessons, whatever those endless possibilities might be. As we open up, release ourselves from resisting what we're working through, we disrupt the patterns we've adopted and allow the pain and fear we might want to cling to, to naturally settle away. We open to the solutions and wisdom that resistance made previously unavailable.

So, in willingly making ourselves available to learn how to love the fearful and painful moments that we're confronted with in life, it allows us to have a fresh point of view to work through. With that new beginning, a space can be made that helps fear and pain more gently settle away, and we're then able to see them as lessons toward truth; they help us to see life with compassion.

Opening to an acceptance of the issues that tend to unfold in life allows us to cultivate a deeper understanding of the nature of fear and an appreciation of the lessons that come forward through its presence. You don't love fear to keep it around; you love the fear that makes its way into your life so that it's free to be seen, it's clear in your mind, presented to the heart, learned from, and then allowed to leave. As Elizabeth Gilbert says, "Fear, you don't have to let it drive the car." To approach fear with more fear and anxiety just creates and multiplies more of the same. Love negates that cycle. When we are presented with fear, it lets us know that there are simply questions in life that need to be answered, so patiently, we open to the answers.

Fear just wants understanding and the acknowledgment that it has lessons to teach. It really doesn't want to stick around, and it can only do so if it's invited to.

JOURNEY PROMPT

Here's your homework! Read this a couple more times today and watch how it shifts inside you as things appear for you to apply it to. And take notes so you can go back there.

> *"The most beautiful people we have known are those who have known defeat, known suffering, known struggle, known loss, and have found their way out of the depths. These persons have an appreciation, a sensitivity and an understanding of life that fills them with compassion, gentleness, and a deep loving concern. Beautiful people do not just happen."*
> *-Elizabeth Kubler-Ross*

Everybody has moments in their lives when they want to blame other people, politics, religion, parents, family, friends and enemies alike, anything and anyone for their problems. It seems like we get stuck in a mindset where we feel compelled to play victim to situations that seem overwhelming, confusing, or difficult. It's hard to avoid this when you feel like life hasn't been treating you fairly. And we tend to react when we're confronted with unfair circumstances—the encounters that keep us wrestling in our heads and in our hearts. How long we stay in our victimhood varies, and, more importantly, it's a voluntary thing. We tend to want to strike out, blame others for how we feel. We feel like we need someone or something to take the fall for our pain, believing that life would be different if it wasn't for them or that event.

What we need to acknowledge is that, in all the blaming, we've forgotten who we really are because we've tried to find our strength through our assumed role as the victim. Obviously, getting stuck in the blame game is inherently misguided. No matter how hard we try to fix or find justice around the issues we're in a funk about, we need to recognize *this: If we view ourselves as "weak," "less than," or "powerless" because of outside influences, then we've taken on the role of victim! We've become victims of our own thinking, not our circumstance. That's a quality of thought which serves no one. It's misdirected thinking that demands a re-boot directly back into your healthy power.*

If our thought directs us into pain without the possibility for healing, then our thinking is going to be darn unproductive, and will only serve to keep us down. Your movement forward lays in your ability to shift the quality of thinking about the truth of who you are. Shift into thinking that incorporates your self-love and personal power; thinking that opens the door to fresh understanding, forgiveness potential for everyone, including yourself, and a quality that brings an emotional health that flows through a loving heart.

Recognizing THE GIFTS IN THE WOUND

Whatever your injury, addiction, or suffering may look like, believe that *you can heal*; know that *you're made to heal*. This is true for the body, mind, and the spirit. They're all designed to heal automatically and with or without our participation, although our belief in ourselves and our innate abilities seem to greatly facilitate the process.

JOURNEY PROMPT

Think about it: What would be the point of believing that you can't heal? Would your disbelief in yourself create any benefit for you or anyone around you?

In all events, past, present and to come, there are always deeper messages and plenty of lessons to be seen if you allow them to emerge. Be open to the hidden meaning in your life because there's a lot of growth and wisdom that can arise from it. Give yourself the permission to open to your past and present pain and see into its potential lessons. Be aware that when we get stuck in our thinking about what's wrong or how something has to be different, we can lose its deeper message… unless, of course, the message is, *"You have to get stuck in this and overthink it!"* but fortunately, that's usually not the case.

Recognizing THE GIFTS IN THE WOUND

JOURNEY PROMPT

Think of an event that you've resisted in some way, maybe even passionately resisted, only to find that you've learned some of your most profound life lessons through. If you can't think of anything, go in reverse. Consider a lesson you've learned in life and trace it back to the situation that set you up for it. Now, take a minute and write a little about them.

Take a note:

Situation:

Lesson:

Situation:

Growth:

ROSCOE

"Perhaps all the dragons in our lives are princesses who are only waiting to see us act, just once, with beauty and courage. Perhaps everything that frightens us is, in its deepest essence, something helpless that wants our love."
-Rilke

Not all gifts come wrapped up nice and pretty.

Do your best to receive all that life offers you graciously. There may be moments that you really don't feel like celebrating, but there is always a gift to be had in living and, often, the greatest part of that gift lays in your reception of it. So, allow the gift, no matter the wrapping. Because even when it's hard, it's perfect.

Everyone puts peace-cultivating life lessons in front of us. They may look other than "peace-filled," but be sure, they all do, indeed, hold great rewards.

Even in your cloudiest moments, *a path forward still exists.*

JOURNEY PROMPT

"Hard times are often blessings in disguise. Let go and let life strengthen you. No matter how much it hurts, hold your head up and keep going. This is an important lesson to remember when you're having a rough day, a bad month, or a crappy year. Truth be told, sometimes the hardest lessons to learn are the ones your spirit needs most. Your past was never a mistake if you learned from it. So, take all the crazy experiences and lessons and place them in a box labeled 'Thank you.'"
-Manisha Shrestha Bundela

"Have patience. All things are difficult before they become easy."
-Saadi

It's hard for anyone to be patient with the process of this journey. Ironically, one of the most important things we can learn is… patience with the process! How odd. Guess it's a pretty big deal! Tricky little universe!

www.ingramcontent.com/pod-product-compliance
Lightning Source LLC
Chambersburg PA
CBHW021432070526
44577CB00001B/175